# LOTS OF THINGS TO KNOW ABOUT ROBOTS

James Maclaine
and Laura Cowan

Illustrated by
Susanna Rumiz

Designed by
Ella Hood and Katie Goldwren

With expert advice from Professor Helge Wurdemann,
Professor of Robotics, University College London

## USBORNE QUICKLINKS

Scan this code for links to websites where you can see robots in action, or go to **usborne.com/Quicklinks** and type in the title of this book.

Usborne Publishing is not responsible for the content of external websites. Children should be supervised online.

Did you know that you can buy kits to build and program your own robots?

What does PROGRAM mean?

You can check the meaning of that word in the glossary on page 62. And there's an index on pages 63-64 to help you search for a topic.

# Robots as old as grandparents

Robots are types of machines. Say hello to some of the **first** ones ever invented...

We were built in the year 1949.

We could find our way around a room.

NAMES: ELMER AND ELSIE

There were only a few robots about 70 years ago. It took lots of time, effort and mistakes to make them.

I started working in a factory in 1961.

WHOOSH

NAME: UNIMATE

The scientists who made me between 1966 and 1972 gave me my name because I wobbled.

NAME: SHAKEY

WHIRRRR

Nowadays, the number of robots around the world has grown to many **millions**.

# What makes a robot a ROBOT?

If all kinds of robots came together to have their picture taken, you'd see how different they look.

So, what do they have in common?

**1.** Every robot can **move**.

I'm fixed to this spot but my claw bends in all directions.

I roll from place to place on wheels.

My four spinning propellers let me fly.

I can swim.

Remember to look at the camera, please!

# How are robots made?

The people who design, build and test out robots are called **roboticists**. Without them, there would be no robots.

Every robot starts out as a bright idea...

Decorating cakes neatly is TRICKY. Could this be a job for a robot?

Maybe. Let's get to work.

At first, roboticists come up with designs and do calculations on a computer.

Then they build models.

They might use a 3D printer to print all the hard, soft and bendy parts needed — in any shape.

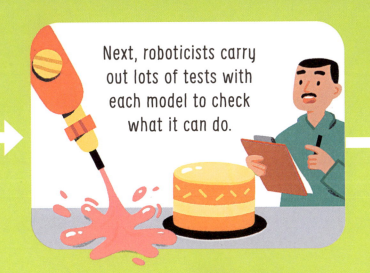

Next, roboticists carry out lots of tests with each model to check what it can do.

If it doesn't work, they try again and again, making changes until it does.

Success.

If the new type of robot is easy enough to produce, lots more might be made.

Sometimes, other robots help.

We're robots building robots.

One day, these new robots might be available for people to buy.

MY CAKE MATE 500

NEW

But most new robots are used in experiments. They stay in roboticists' labs.

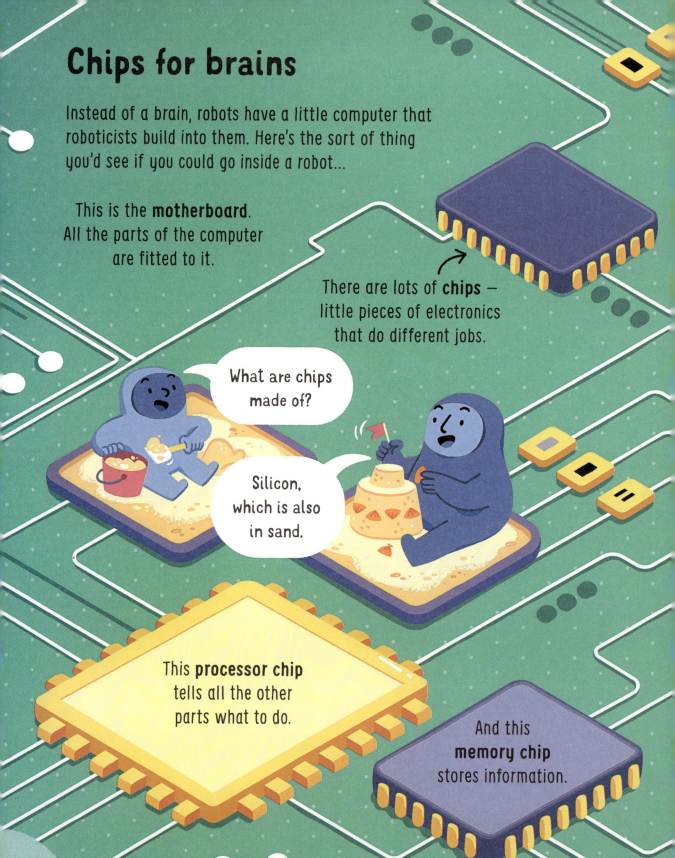

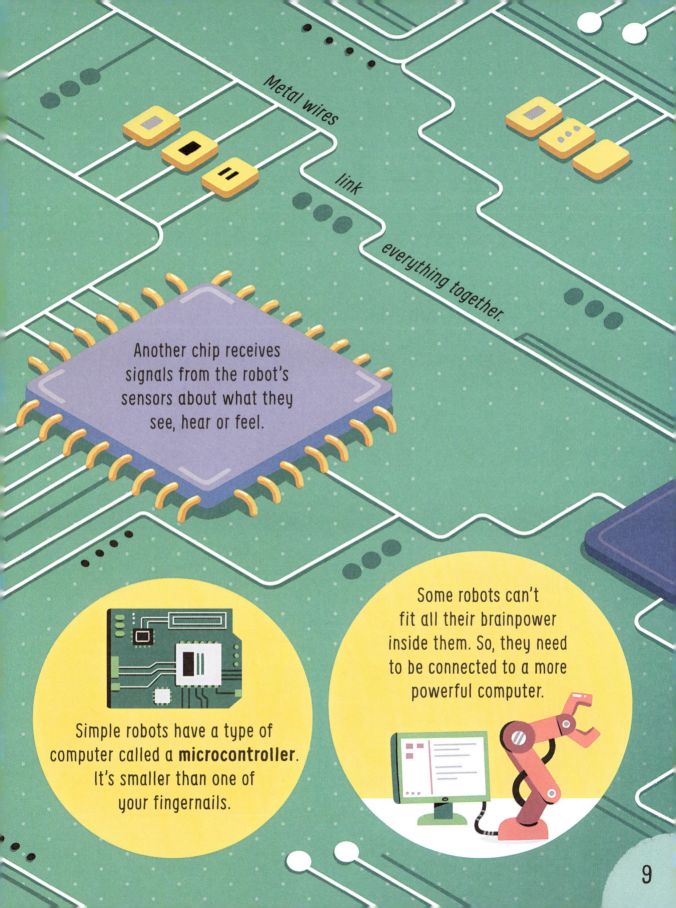

Metal wires link everything together.

Another chip receives signals from the robot's sensors about what they see, hear or feel.

Simple robots have a type of computer called a **microcontroller**. It's smaller than one of your fingernails.

Some robots can't fit all their brainpower inside them. So, they need to be connected to a more powerful computer.

# Step by step, by step, by step...

Instructions for robots need to be explained very, very carefully — even for tasks that might seem simple to you.

Imagine you ask a robot to wrap a present. These are just some of the questions it would need answering first:

Roboticists think through the answers before breaking the task down into a list of step-by-step rules and instructions. The list is known as an **algorithm**.

# The only numbers that robots need

For a robot's computer to follow an algorithm, it has to be turned into a type of language called **machine code**. It's made up of lots and lots of 0s and 1s.

At a glance, machine code looks very repetitive, but it's not. The exact order of the numbers tells the robot **everything** it needs to do — and **when** to do it.

# Getting smarter

Some robots are smart enough to do things that you and your brain can. They can...

...decide what to do

I will...

...make guesses

I think...

...and come up with some ideas.

How about...?

These sorts of robots have something called **AI**. The letters stand for **artificial intelligence**.

For a robot to have AI, its computer needs **many** algorithms. Some of the algorithms use lots of information, called **data**, to **learn** in different ways.

To help a robot learn, AI scientists give its computer thousands of examples of similar things.

Later, the robot learns to recognize them.

That's a CLOCK!

The robot can also test things on its own to work out what they do.

When it sees similar things, it can use them.

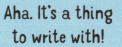

Aha. It's a thing to write with!

Did you know that these were both the ways you learned when you were very young?

Clock, clock...

# Why robots are like bats

Some robots are as **noisy** as bats – but you can't hear either of them.

When a bat is hunting moths, it makes sounds that are too high for people to hear.

*Now I know where you are...*

If the sounds hit something, they bounce back to the bat's ears. This helps it to find where a moth is flying.

# How robots smell

Different types of sensors can even help robots to detect **smells**.

When gassy smells drift into this robot's sensor, it sends a signal to its computer.

**CHEMICAL SENSOR**

*Sniff, sniff... LEAKING GAS! Someone needs to fix that pipe.*

A robot fitted with an **ultrasonic sensor** makes sounds just as high as a bat.

**ULTRASONIC SENSOR**

The sounds tell the robot when things are nearby. Then it changes direction to avoid crashing into them.

Something ahead!

**Chemical sensors** only react to the smells they're designed to find. Nothing happens when other smells reach them.

Your nose is a much better sensor. It can tell over a **trillion** smells apart.

Why can't I smell those flowers?

You'd need a LOT more sensors to smell them all, robot!

# Arms just like yours

Try bending your arm up, down and from side to side. Next, turn it one way and then the other too. Many robots have parts that move like this. They're called **robotic arms**.

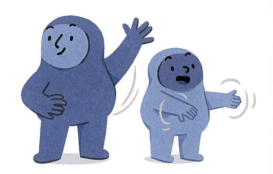

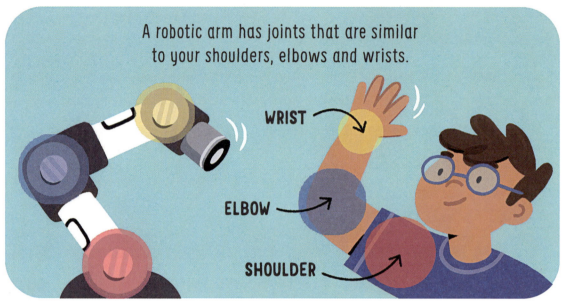

A robotic arm has joints that are similar to your shoulders, elbows and wrists.

**WRIST**

**ELBOW**

**SHOULDER**

Because they're so flexible, robotic arms are very useful in...

...science labs      ...factories      ...and space.

They pick up tubes of chemicals to do experiments.

They help pack things into crates and boxes.

Astronauts ride a giant robotic arm when doing spacewalks.

# Super hands

Your hands are amazing. They can do all sorts of things: tie shoelaces, roll dough into a ball, grip onto bike handles, gently stroke a baby chick...

Designing a **robotic hand** that can do as much as you is a tough challenge for roboticists.

So far, robotic hands can...

...use scissors.

(But they can't cut out fiddly shapes.)

...pick up tiny things with tweezers.

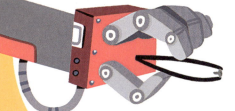

(But they can only do it slowly.)

...grasp a container.

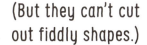

(But they can't open the lid.)

...hold an egg.

(But they might crack it... or drop it.)

Don't worry. Making mistakes helps robots' computers learn how to do better next time.

# Power for robots

Robots need power from **electricity** to work. Without it, they can't sense things or move, and their computers won't function.

Lots of robots have **batteries** inside them. But, eventually, they use up all the power.

So that they don't need new batteries again and again, some robots are **plugged in** to recharge.

Robots on wheels can drive to a **charging station** when their batteries need topping up.

Time for an energy boost!

If robots are fixed to the same spot, they don't need batteries. They have **cables** that supply them with electricity non-stop.

Robots that work outdoors might use **solar panels** that turn sunlight into power.

In 2004, roboticists fitted an unusual type of battery into a little robot called **EcoBot II**.

Its battery could break down rotting plums, pears or peaches to make electricity.

19

# Car builders

There are more than a **million** robots at work in car factories around the world. They help out at every stage, in ways that are quick, safe and reliable...

Then painting robots spray fine layers of paint over the metal until it's bright and shiny.

"We're here to fix the robots if they break down."

**3**

**4**

When the paint is dry, another robot checks the body all over.

**5**

More robots fit the engine, windows and wheels.

**6**

And now this robot screws in the lights to add the finishing touches.

21

# Copying cats and other creatures

When inventing robots, roboticists sometimes look to amazing animals for new ideas.

**CHEETAH**

This type of big cat is the fastest runner on Earth.

**MINI CHEETAH**

Roboticists investigated the way a cheetah's legs move to build a robot that can sprint.

**SLOTH**

The leaves that a sloth eats give it very little energy. But it moves very slowly so it doesn't need much.

**SLOTHBOT**

SlothBot moves slowly too and it only needs sunlight to power it.

It can study forests without disturbing wildlife.

**OCTOPUS**

The body and eight arms of an octopus are soft. It can fit itself into all kinds of narrow places.

Most robots are hard, but Octobot is as squishy as an octopus.

**OCTOBOT**

That's why it can squeeze into tight spots to explore.

**PEREGRINE FALCON**

There's no bird speedier than a peregrine falcon — and it can grab onto any surface without slipping.

**SNAG**

Roboticists copied the falcon's feet and claws to help SNAG take off and land with just as much skill.

# Awwww...

Some robots have faces, voices and body parts like humans have. They're known as **humanoid robots**.

The robots you see in cartoons are often humanoid robots.

In the real world, they're used in offices, museums and hospitals.

They can welcome and entertain visitors — and some can even answer questions.

Big round eyes make humanoid robots look cute and friendly.

Hello. How may I help you?

# ARGGHHH...

Roboticists have built a few humanoid robots that look very realistic. But many people find them a little creepy.

The robots can be covered with skinlike material.

They can make faces to look happy, sad or shocked.

They might be dressed in clothes.

Scientists think that if a robot looks too human, people see it as a strange-looking person instead of a robot. That's why it makes them feel uneasy.

I can't look much longer...

That's OK. There are cuter robots on the next page.

# SNEEZE-FREE PETS

For anyone who wants a pet but can't have one, **companion robots** could be the answer.

These sorts of robots look like real animals or imaginary creatures.

Their bodies move as if they're breathing and their tails wag.

*Please hold me tight!*

**WITH 5 WAGGING SPEEDS**

Companion robots don't need as much care as a cat or dog. But they do purr when their sensors feel someone cuddling them.

**NO-STRESS BUNNY**

*Do these robots ever need to go to the vet?*

*Never! But a roboticist could fix them if something goes wrong.*

ROBO-PETS FOR SALE

Pet fur makes some people's eyes itch or their nose run. Robotic pets are soft and cuddly without this problem.

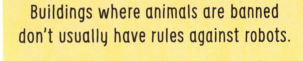
THE FLUFFIEST ROBOT EVER!

Buildings where animals are banned don't usually have rules against robots.

Meow – my sensors can hear voices.

WELCOME ANYWHERE AND EVERYWHERE

Some owners feel less lonely thanks to their robots. They can talk to them when no one else is around.

Scientists have found that these sorts of robots make people happier.

# Chess grandmasters versus robots

In games of chess, computers and robots are **smarter** than humans.

Computers with powerful AI can work out the **best** possible move each turn by doing millions of calculations in a second. That's why even chess champions, known as grandmasters, can't beat them.

The computer can be connected to a robotic arm that works like this...

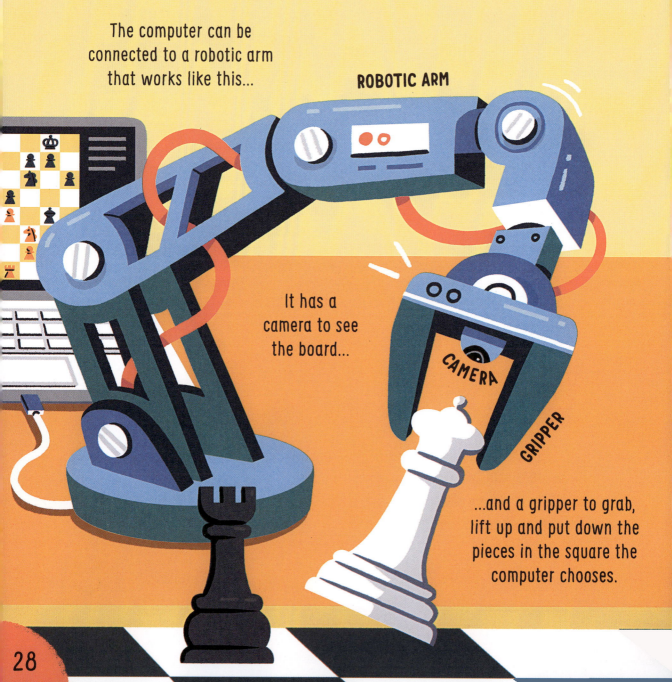

**ROBOTIC ARM**

It has a camera to see the board...

**CAMERA**

**GRIPPER**

...and a gripper to grab, lift up and put down the pieces in the square the computer chooses.

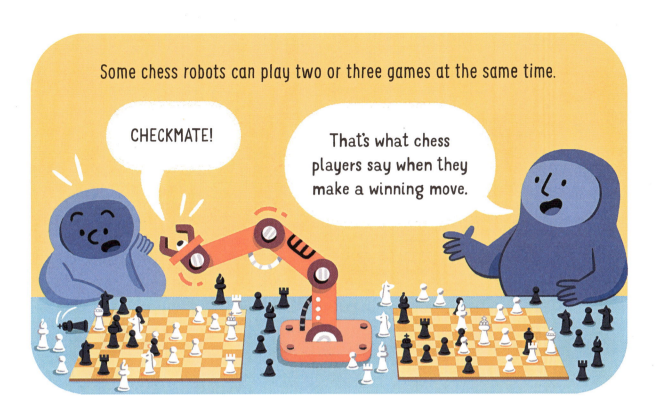

# Robots in the skies

Up, up, up and away! Some robots zip and zoom around the sky. They're called **drones**.

Drones never carry passengers, but they do deliver packages. Speeding through the air, they dodge any traffic jams on the ground.

Drones can fly above dangerous places to film what's happening.

Check out this erupting volcano!

There are drones smaller than butterflies. They can float on the breeze.

If hikers get lost, drones have a bird's-eye view to spot them, so rescuers know where to go.

Phew – help is on the way.

# Weatherdrones

Drones can fly as high as the clouds to send information about the weather to scientists on the ground.

# The robots that do chores

People can keep their homes clean without lifting a finger. These robots do the dirty work instead.

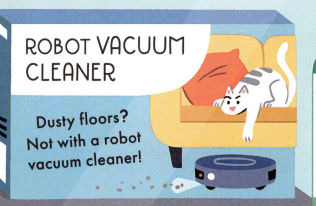

The robot vacuum senses its way around a room, sucking up all the crumbs and dirt it meets.

This robot clings onto windows and moves from corner to corner, removing any streaks.

After spraying soapy liquid, this mopping robot wipes the floor with pads on its base.

Robots can help out with chores outdoors too.

A cable hidden under the ground tells this mower to change direction when it reaches the edges of the lawn.

This pool cleaning robot traps any floating leaves and polishes the tiles.

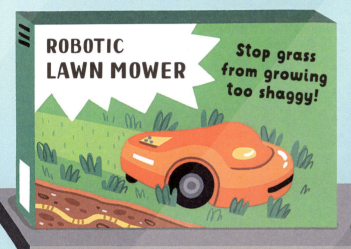

ROBOTIC LAWN MOWER

Stop grass from growing too shaggy!

ROBOTIC POOL CLEANER

It works above AND below water.

All these robots are very good at doing one type of chore again and again. But they can't do lots of different things at once.

There isn't a single robot that could pick up toys, put back books, fold clothes and sort through mess... at least, not yet.

You'll have to clean up your room on your own. No robot can help you!

# Robots before there were robots

Did you know that the word **robot** was invented in the year 1920 — before the first robots were made?

Czech artist Josef Čapek came up with the word for his brother Karel's new play...

The play is about an imaginary factory where machines that look like people are produced.

It would be another 50 years before this happened in real life.

# Taking the stage

Lots more plays — and movies and TV shows too — have featured robot characters. Almost always, actors dress up in costumes or record their voices to portray them.

# Beep beep! Coming through!

In more and more places around the world, fleets of delivery robots are dropping off people's food.

These robots wheel their way along footpaths.

How do they cross a road? They can't reach the button, but they can ask for help...

*Bingly bingly beep! Would you mind pressing the button, please? Thank you.*

The robots also deliver packages and meals.

*Lunch will stay nice and hot in here.*

*Watch out for the dog...*

They have **twelve** cameras to sense things all around them.

# Can't do it

Some jobs are much too **dangerous** for most workers... except for robots.

HARMFUL WASTE TO SORT

Power stations, science labs and hospitals all produce waste that's **radioactive**. This means it releases tiny dangerous particles as the waste breaks down.

Stand well back.

HAZARD

RADIOACTIVE

Coming too close to the particles can make people very sick.

But robots don't get hurt. They collect radioactive waste and store it away safely.

# Won't do it

Robots don't make a fuss when it comes to doing jobs most people would find **revolting**...

**CLOGGED SEWER PIPE TO UNBLOCK**

*I'm not going near that – even in my overalls.*

This great lump of fat, gunk and baby wipes is known as a fatberg.

*Let me at it!*

Sewer robots can fire high-powered jets of water to blast through blockages.

# Intrepid space explorers

NASA (the National Aeronautics and Space Administration) is working on all kinds of robot explorers to send to planets in our solar system.

No one knows what perils they might face, but nothing will stop these brave robots — they could go **anywhere!**

### AEROBOT
One day, this robotic balloon could be ready to scout the planet Venus from the clouds.

### LEMUR 3

This little robot is learning to climb any cliff, however high or steep.

**EELS**

EELS is a snake-shaped robot that wriggles into cracks and holes to scan for signs of life.

**NEBULA-SPOT**

Just like a rescue dog, NeBula-Spot can scramble over rocks and ice, and always knows how to find its way back.

**BRUIE**

BRUIE has two wheels that enable it to roll upside down underneath ice sheets, to explore frozen lakes and seas.

# Do robots follow rules?

Over 80 years ago, American writer Isaac Asimov came up with a set of rules for the robots in his stories. They're known as the **Three Laws of Robotics**.

They command...

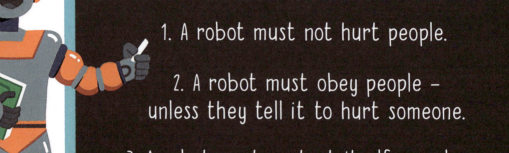

1. A robot must not hurt people.

2. A robot must obey people – unless they tell it to hurt someone.

3. A robot must protect itself – so long as it doesn't harm anyone – unless people order it not to protect itself.

In the real world today, there aren't any official rules for robots. Robots just do what roboticists program them to do.

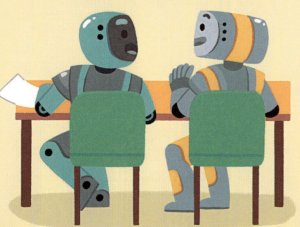

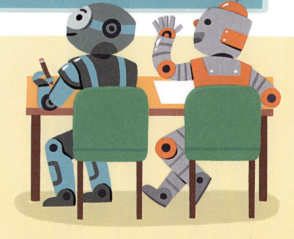

But some people still think about Asimov's Three Laws – and believe there should be rules to control how robots are used.

# Who's to blame?

**Self-driving cars** are robots that have got lots of people thinking. These cars don't need drivers. They have **AI** to tell them how to drive and where to go. So, whose fault is it if an accident happens?

What if a self-driving car reverses into a tree...

Is the **car** to blame?

...or its **owner**?

...or the **passengers**?

Oh no. Poor tree.

...or the **companies** that made the car or designed the AI?

...or even the **tree**?

Hey, I couldn't move out of the way. I'm rooted to this spot.

In countries around the world, the people updating laws for self-driving cars are wondering about these sorts of questions as they decide what to do.

# Teamwork

Little robots that work with each other are called **swarm robots**. Their name comes from the word for a big crowd of insects doing things together.

All the robots in a swarm have the same set of instructions.

*Search out snapped wire!*

Their sensors can tell when another robot is nearby, so they don't bump into each other.

*Time to turn left.*

Even if one of the robots stops working, the rest can carry on with the job.

*Keep going – don't worry about me.*

One day, swarm robots could be sent inside machines to investigate faults.

*Found it!*

Swarm robots could help with building things, too.

TERMES swarm robots can pick up building blocks and stack them on top of each other.

They move and climb on **whegs** — sets of short legs that turn like wheels.

Roboticists at Harvard University created us in 2014.

TERMES ROBOT

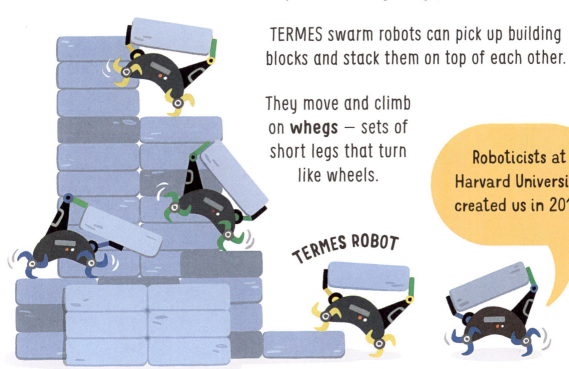

TERMES robots were designed to behave like **termites**.

These tiny insects pile up mud, little by little, to make great mounds above their nests.

Two heads are better than one...

...and thousands of heads are even better.

45

# Clockwork birds and dolls

Long before computers and chips were invented, there were robotlike machines called **automata**. They can move as if they're alive and do all sorts of surprising things.

**CUCKOO CLOCK**

A little automaton bird pops outs of the clock every hour and calls out...

CUCKOO, CUCKOO

Made in Germany, before 1780

**MAILLARDET'S AUTOMATON**

By guiding its pen across a piece of paper, this automaton can write out three poems and draw four pictures with amazing details.

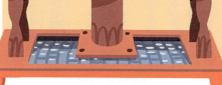

Made in England, around 1800

Wow – look at the ship it drew!

## SILVER SWAN

With a swing of its neck, this swan appears to catch a little fish.

Made in England, before 1774

## TEA-SERVING DOLL

When a cup of tea is placed onto its tray, this doll starts walking until someone takes the cup.

Made in Japan, 1796

## HOW DO AUTOMATA WORK?

If you could look inside, you'd see all these automata are powered by the same types of parts as old clocks.

SPRING

GEARS

Winding up the spring makes the gears turn so the clock or automaton starts to move.

47

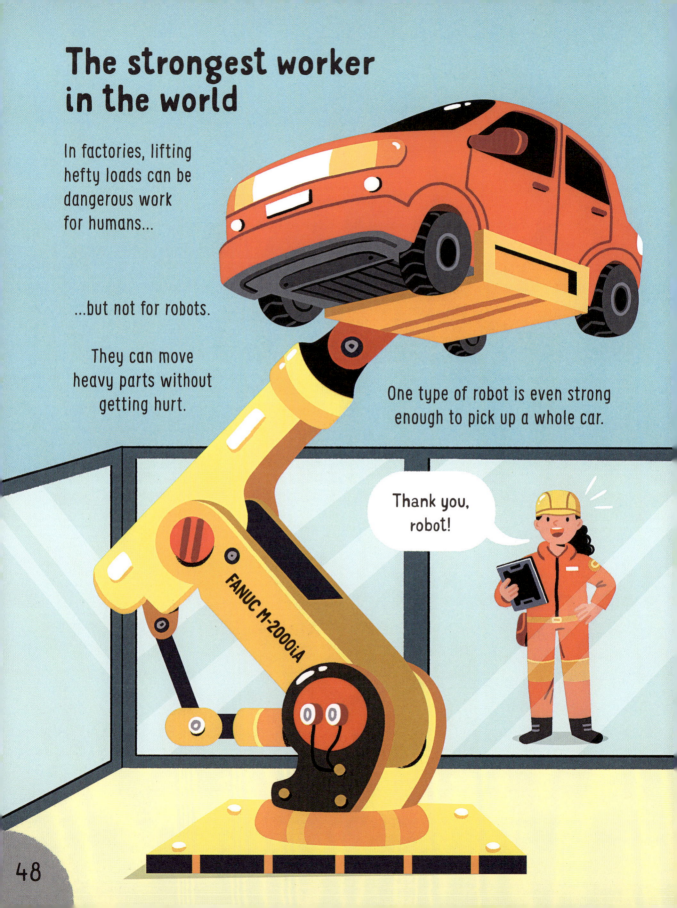

# The strongest worker in the world

In factories, lifting hefty loads can be dangerous work for humans...

...but not for robots.

They can move heavy parts without getting hurt.

One type of robot is even strong enough to pick up a whole car.

Thank you, robot!

# Mini but MIGHTY

Could you lug a rhino up a climbing wall? Well, this little robot named MicroTug knows what it's like to carry something that's so much heavier than itself.

MICROTUG

The robot is about the size of a cherry, but it can climb up a wall, hoisting...

...OVER 100 TIMES ITS OWN WEIGHT!

Climbing is hard enough without carrying stuff, too.

The amazing way that MicroTug clings onto the wall was inspired by small lizards called geckos.

I have tiny hairs on my toes that help me grip. MicroTug has similar hairs on its base.

# Grown by robots

Not all farmers are humans. There are robots that work in fields and giant greenhouses to grow and harvest all types of food.

# The bees that don't buzz

Bumble, Honey and Queen sound like good names for bees, but they're actually three robots working with astronauts in space. Built by NASA, they're known as **Astrobees**.

They can film experiments inside a space station...

QUEEN

Ready for your close-up?

...check the air is safe to breathe...

All fresh!

BUMBLE

...and seek out problems.

HONEY

Has someone lost a sock?

WHIRRRR

Astrobees are as big as basketballs. They can fly thanks to electric fans that spin inside them. They do make whirring sounds — but there's no buzzing.

# Dancing for bees

Back on Earth, roboticists are testing out different kinds of robots that could help **honey bees**. They're struggling to find enough food.

Connected by a rod to a motor, one bee-sized robot can go inside the place where the bees live. It's called a hive.

RoboBee dances in circles. The pattern it makes shows the bees where to look for food outside the hive.

OOOH – tasty flowers on the other side of the field.

Let's fly there now!

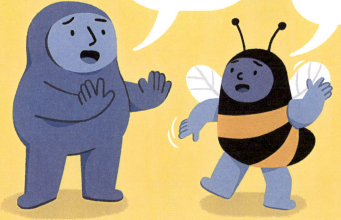

The bees don't need YOU to dance.

Sorry.

Real honey bees do this sort of dance to tell each other about places with new flowers or water to drink. RoboBee could help them find more.

Robots help out on roads in Singapore, too.

Meanwhile in America, robots make sure bridges are safe to drive on. There are over 617,000 bridges to check, and some of them are very old.

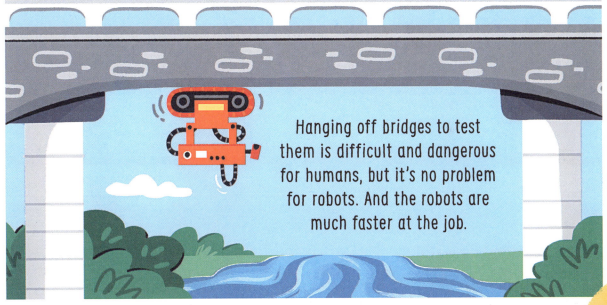

Hanging off bridges to test them is difficult and dangerous for humans, but it's no problem for robots. And the robots are much faster at the job.

# Wearable robots

Coming down this runway are some of the most amazing things people can wear. They're known as **robot suits**.

Some robot suits help people who can't walk on their own.

Sensors in the suit detect tiny movements in the person's legs. Then **motors** start to power their stride.

← MOTOR

Several straps fit the suit close to the body.

**Robotic boots** can be worn over ordinary shoes. They help someone walk faster for longer.

# Mysteries of the deep

On a trip down, down, down to the deepest parts of the world's oceans, you might spy robots at work.

They're making all kinds of discoveries.

"Look there, below us!"

This robot explorer is known as a **remotely operated vehicle** — or **ROV** for short.

Very long cables take electricity to the ROV. They also send back pictures and information from its travels.

"Nobody has seen an octopus like this before."

ROV

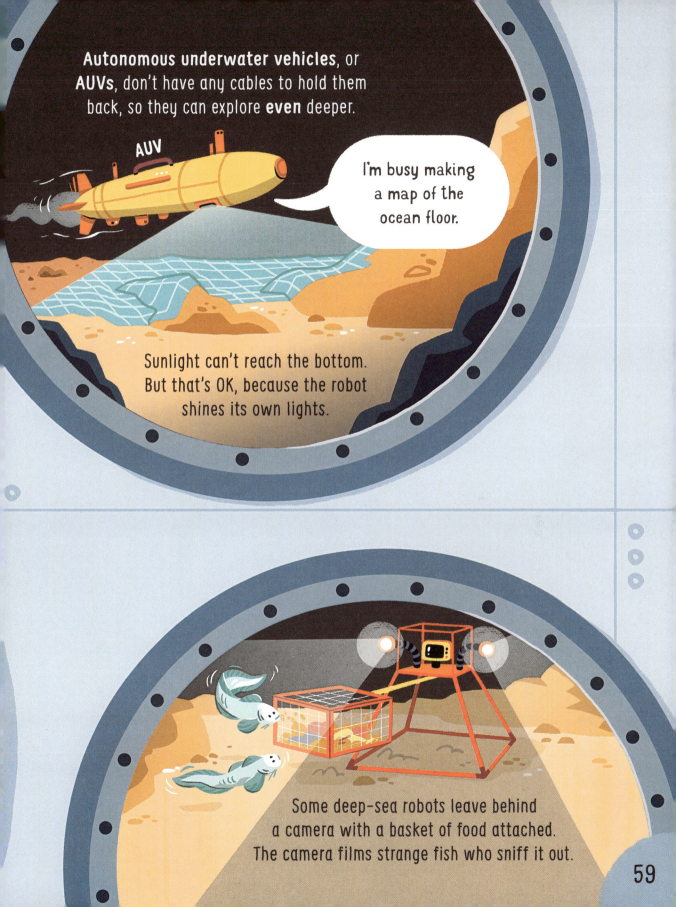

# Ever-shrinking robots

Roboticists are designing smaller and smaller robots. There are different names for them according to their tininess.

## MILLIROBOT

Each type of robot is no bigger than the black square next to its name.

Even though it's just the size of a pea, this **millirobot** can move around in different places — even underwater.

## MICROROBOT ·

This isn't a speck of dust on the page of your book. It's a **microrobot**.

It's shaped like a crab and thin enough to scuttle through the eye of a needle.

## NANOROBOT

I can't make out any robot or square here...

A **nanorobot** is far too little to see. It's over 100 times narrower than one of the hairs on your head.

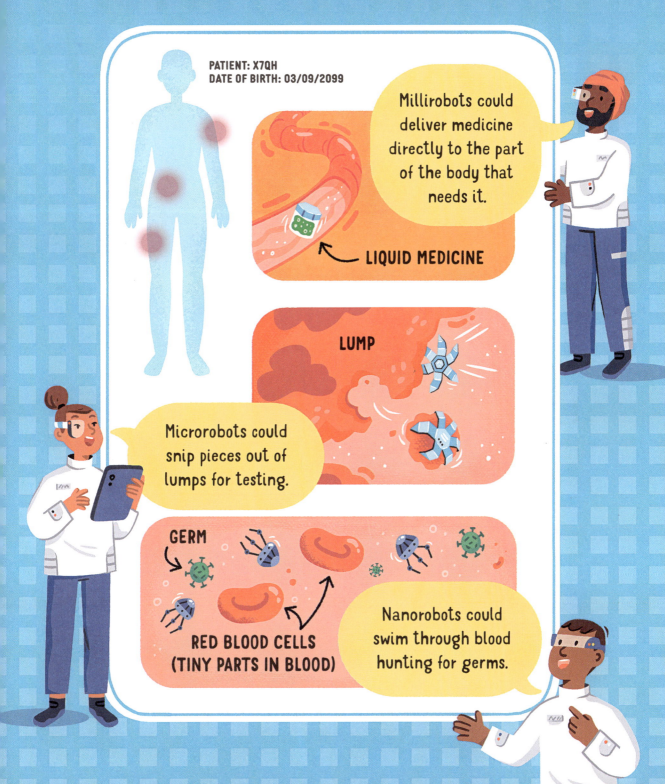

# Glossary

Here you can find out what some of the words in this book *mean*...

*algorithm* – a list of instructions or rules for a **computer**

*artificial intelligence (AI)* – the ability of a computer or robot to do things that you and your brain can

*automaton* – a type of machine that moves or does things on its own

*battery* – a container of chemicals that produces **electricity**

*camera* – a machine or part in a robot that takes photographs or records what's around it

*chip* – an **electronic** part that helps make a **computer** work

*code* – a type of language used when writing instructions for a **computer**

*computer* – a machine that processes **data** and carries out tasks

*data* – all of the information stored on or used by a **computer**

*drone* – a type of robot that can fly

*electricity* – a type of energy that powers things to work

*electronic* – any machine that works by using **electricity**

*gear* – a wheel with teeth around its edge that turns in a machine

*microcontroller* – a small type of **computer**

*motherboard* – the hard sheet in a **computer** that holds the **chips** and other parts

*motor* – a part in a machine which uses **electricity** to make it move

*program* – to write instructions for a robot's **computer** in **code**

*roboticist* – a person who designs, builds and tests robots

*sensor* – a part in a robot that feels, hears, sees or detects things and sends information to its **computer**

*solar panel* – a device that turns sunlight into **electricity**

*spring* – a coil of metal that helps make a **gear** turn

*tracker* – an **electronic** device that shows where something is

*wheg* – a set of short legs that turns like a wheel

# Index

algorithms, 10, 11, 13, 62
animals, 22, 23, 26, 27, 45, 49, 53
artificial intelligence (AI), 12-13, 28, 29, 43, 50, 62
astronauts, 16, 52
automata, 46-47, 62
autonomous underwater vehicles (AUVs), 59

bats, 14, 15
batteries, 18, 19, 62
bees, 52, 53
bridges, 55

cameras, 28, 30, 36, 50, 54, 59, 62
cars, 20, 21, 43, 48, 54, 55
charging stations, 18
cheetahs, 22
chess, 28-29
chips, 8, 62
cleaning, 5, 32-33
climbing, 40, 45, 49, 55
clocks, 46, 47
code, 11, 62
companion robots, 26-27
computers, 5, 6, 8-9, 13, 17, 18, 28, 62

data, 13, 62
delivery robots, 30, 36-37

doctors, 61
drawing, 46
drones, 30-31, 51, 62

electricity, 18, 19, 62

factories, 3, 16, 20-21, 48
farms, 50-51
fatberg, 39
flying, 4, 23, 30, 31, 40, 52
food, 36, 37, 50, 51
fruit, 19, 50, 51

gears, 47, 62
geckos, 49
grippers, 28

hives, 53
humanoid robots, 24-25, 54

laws, 42, 43, 55
learning, 13
lifting, 16, 48, 49, 57

machine code, 11, 62
microcontrollers, 9, 62
microrobots, 60-61
millirobots, 60-61
motherboards, 8, 9, 62
motors, 53, 56, 62
moving, 4, 15, 16, 17, 18, 22, 23, 32, 33, 35, 40, 41, 44, 45, 46, 47, 49, 53, 55, 56, 60, 61

nanorobots, 60-61
NASA, 40-41, 52

oceans, 58, 59
octopuses, 23, 58

peregrine falcons, 23
pets, 26, 27
plays, 34, 35
program, 2, 42, 62

radioactive waste, 38
remotely operated vehicles (ROVs), 58
roads, 54-55
robot suits, 56-57
robotic arms, 16, 28, 29, 48
robotic boots, 56
robotic combine harvesters, 51
robotic hands, 17
roboticists, 6-7, 8, 10, 17, 22, 23, 26, 42, 60, 62

science labs, 7, 16
seas, 41, 58, 59
self-driving cars, 43
sensors, 5, 9, 14-15, 18, 26, 31, 26, 27, 44, 56, 62
sewers, 39
sloths, 22

63

sloths, 22
smells, 14, 15
solar panels, 19, 22, 54, 62
sounds, 14, 15, 26, 27, 52
space, 16, 40-41, 52
space stations, 52
springs, 47, 62
swarm robots, 44-45
swimming, 4, 60, 61

talking, 24, 35, 36
termites, 45
Three Laws of Robotics, the, 42
trackers, 37, 62
traffic, 30, 54, 55

vegetables, 51

walking, 56
weather, 31
wheels, 4, 18, 36, 41, 51
whegs, 45, 62
writing, 46

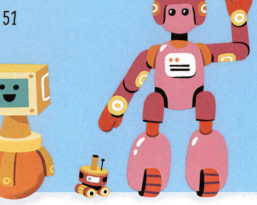

Series editor: Ruth Brocklehurst
Series designer: Helen Lee

The publisher is grateful to the following roboticists and organizations for permission to feature their robots:
**pp20-21** KUKA Robotics; **p22 (top)** Professor Sangbae Kim; **p22 (bottom)** Magnus Egerstedt; **p23 (top)** Jennifer Lewis and Robert Wood, Harvard University; **p23 (bottom)** Will Roderick, Dept. of Mechanical Engineering, Stanford University; **p32** Engineered Arts; **pp36-37** Starship Technologies Ltd; **p45** Professor Radhika Nagpal; **p48** FANUC; **p49** Biomimetics and Dexterous Manipulation Lab, Stanford University; **p53** Professor Dr. Tim Landgraf; **p54** Thérèse Kirongozi, CEO of Women's Technologies; **p60 (top)** R. Renee Zhao, Stanford University.

With thanks to Ehimare Ogona

First published in 2024 by Usborne Publishing Limited, 83-85 Saffron Hill, London EC1N 8RT, United Kingdom. usborne.com Copyright © 2024 Usborne Publishing Limited. The name Usborne and the Balloon logo are registered trade marks of Usborne Publishing Limited. All rights reserved. No part of this publication may be reproduced, stored in a retrieval system or transmitted in any form or by any means without prior permission of the publisher. First published in America 2025. UE.

Please follow the online safety guidelines at usborne.com/Quicklinks